GUIDE TO THE *Municipal House*

1|

1| *Stairway from the ground floor*

FROM THE MIDDLE AGES TO THE PRESENT

King's Court

The history of the site where Prague's Municipal House now stands is both interesting and complex. The adjacent Powder Gate, a unique fragment of Prague's Old Town fortifications dating from the Gothic period, recalls the times when an important trade route arrived at this point. This was probably only one of many reasons why King Wenceslas IV. decided in the late 14th century to establish his residence in this area, beside the fortification walls. The residence was given the name **King's Court**.

The site also served Bohemian rulers during the unsettled times of the Hussite revolution, and was finally abandoned only when Vladislav II of the Jagellon dynasty left the place and moved back to Prague Castle. As late as 1475 however, King Vladislav personally laid a foundation stone for a new gate that was to be built in the fortification wall to replace the previous one which was so run-down it had been

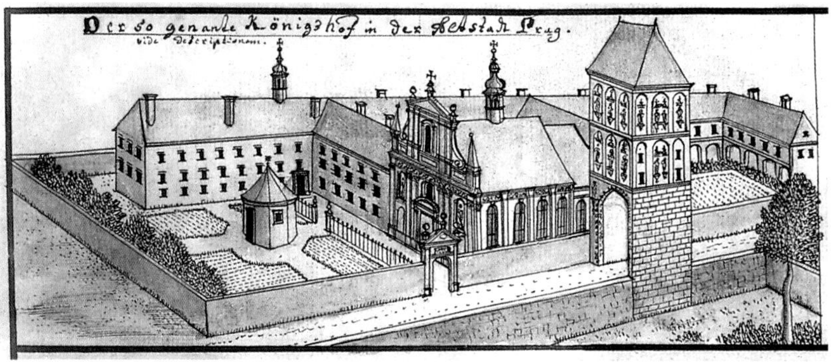

| 2

2 | *Friedrich Bernhard Werner: The Royal Court near the Powder Tower, drawing (c. 1740)*

3 | 

nicknamed the "Ragged Gate".

The Hapsburgs who began their reign in Bohemia in 1526 were no longer interested in the King's Court and left the former royal residence unoccupied. The empty and deteriorating palace was purchased in 1631 by Cardinal Arnošt Harrach from Polyxena of Lobkowitz, who established an **archiepiscopal seminary** there. Following a fire in 1689 the complex was rebuilt and remodelled, and **St. Vojtěch's Church** was added.

At that time the gate was used as a storage place for gun-powder and that's how it later got its name — Powder Gate or Powder Tower. In 1776 the seminary was moved to the Klementinum and King's Court was then used by the military who converted it into a barracks. In the late 19th century this building later became a **military academy**.

The turn of the 19th and 20th centuries in Prague was marked by a mighty wave of sanitation reform and slum-area clearances which were intended to contribute to turning Prague into a modern European city. The King's Court site became a great challenge for the city authorities and the whole complex of the former seminary as well as the St. Vojtěch church were eventually torn down. A year later, the small shops that had stood to the east of the Powder Tower were also demolished.

3 | *Jindřich Eckert: View of the Powder Tower from the east, small shops to the right of the tower, the cadet school already demolished, 1903*

Design and construction of the Municipal House

The idea of using the former King's Court plot as a site to build an outstanding and representative building for the Czech kingdom's capital was first initiated by a **Prague Civic Society memorandum**, submitted to the Town Hall authorities in 1901. The request proposed the creation of a center for Czech official and social undertakings, citing among other reasons the necessity for a counterbalance to a German casino and the German House (now Slovanský dům — the Slavic House) on Na příkopě Street.

In 1903 an architectural competition took place. Three designs by the architects **Dryák, Pospíšil** and **Balšánek** received awards, but not

4

4 | *Osvald Polívka, Antonín Balšánek: Draft design of the main front facade (version "O"), ink, aquarelle*

even the second round of the competition produced a winning design and so the Prague City Council decided that the architects **Professor Antonín Balšánek** and **Osvald Polívka** would be commissioned for the project. The work was supervised by a nine-member committee which included councillor Prof. Josef Schulz, architect Jiří Stibral and architect Václav Roštlapil.

5

The final design and a 3,000,000 crown budget were finally approved after a series of delays on 10 December 1904, and in the summer of 1905 the firm **Schlaffer & Šebek** began the construction work. Some of the sections were put into use as early as 1909—1910 while the entire building was officially opened on 22 November 1912.

The Municipal House — one of the most remarkable constructions of Prague Art Nouveau. At the time of its creation it was critisized by some architects as its style was considered to be formally outdated.

The lapse of almost a century since then allows us to forget about the emotions and controversy of those times and to appreciate this building as a unique harmony of architectural and painting styles of the turn of the 19th and 20th centuries. Neo-Baroque, Neo-Renaissance, and both Western and Oriental influences fuse together with Czech Art Nouveau. The impression this building gives is enhanced

5 | *Jindřich Eckert: View of the construction site from U Prašné brány Street, 1906*

by a wide range of decorative styles and materials, as well as by the high quality of craftmanship. The monumental appearance of the building is crowned by the outstanding decor created by most of the prominent Czech artists of the day, namely the painters **Mikoláš Aleš, Václav Jansa, Alfons Mucha, Jakub Obrovský, Jan Preisler, Josef Wenig, Karel Špillar, Max Švabinský, Josef Ullman, František Ženíšek,** and the sculptors **Josef Mařatka, Josef Václav Myslbek, Karel Novák, Ladislav Šaloun, František Uprka, Bohumil Kafka** and **Čeněk Vosmík.**

The building was equipped with all the modern facilities of the time, including central heating and ventilation, drinking and utility water-supply system, suction removal of dust, cooling of the cellar, ice-making, electrical as well as hydraulic elevators, steam-powered laundry, laundry drying room, bottle-washing facility, transformer station, accummulator station, tube post and an intercom network.

Total costs amounted to 6,083,000 crowns, the built up area is 4,214 sqm and the volume of the building is 139,176 cubic meters.

The Municipal House has undergone several partial reconstructions. The latest was a thorough renovation and took place between 1994 and 1997.

|6

6 | *Mascaron on the main dome, an allegoric head*

OPEN AIR GALLERY

The Municipal House facade is eye-catching not only due to its monumental architectural composition but also because of the unique profile created by its collection of the sculptural art of the time. Monumental allegorical figures, displayed all over the facade of the building, which were created by some of the greatest artists represent particular historical and classical cultural symbols (allegories of the nation, Prague, legendary characters and events, personification of art, philosophy, science, etc.), but they are also inspired by modern day symbols (allegories of industry, trade, transport). Anthropomorphical sculptures are accompanied by decor with Art Nouveau floral ornaments as well as other classical architectural elements.

|7

Above the tops of attic gables and on the tips of the spires there are sculpted vases, cartouches, tombs, stylized battlements and other decorative elements.

The front facade in line with the cupola axis is dominated by the main entrance portal with a representative semi-circular balcony which is accessible from the Mayor's Hall on the 1st floor.

The large exedra under the main cupola is decorated with a semi-circular scene on the glass colorful mosaic *Apotheosis of Prague* according to a painting by **Karel Špillar**. The picture is adorned with

7 | *Mascaron over a window of the front facade, "Philosophy allegory"*

| 8

a golden sign with a quotation by **Svatopluk Čech** which is still relevant today : *"HAIL TO YOU PRAGUE ! BRAVE THE TIME AND MALICE AS YOU HAVE RESISTED ALL THE STORMS THROUGHOUT THE AGES".*

The Municipal House is special for the mutual harmony of all the decorative elements with architectural features which provide with

8 | *East facade of the Municipal House and the Powder Tower*

9 | 

their shape and form a suitable background for the wonderful sculptural display. Richly ornate, color-verdigried stucco ornaments and artificial stone cover all the facades and continue similarly on the roof in copper, zinc and zinc alloy. All these metalwork elements are, with the exception of the roof area, provided with gilding and ochre paint which is intended to imitate stucco. Some sculptured figures are partly made of stone (sandstone), partly of artificial stone, while others are bronze and copper. The whole monumental look is completed by the painted and gilded, highly decorative metalwork elements of the balcony hand-rail, portal sun roofs, etc.

 | 10

The sculptures on the Municipal House facade were created by a number of renowned artists of the day. Two central stone sculptural groups called *Humiliation and Revival of the Nation* (featuring a copper eagle), placed alongside the central cupola's exedra were created by **Ladislav Šaloun. Karel**

9 | *Memorial plaque commemorating the events of 1918 (Ladislav Šaloun)*

10 | *Torch-bearer on the main sun roof (by Karel Novák)*

11 | 

Novák created a pair of huge copper atlas figures — torch-bearers carrying the *"Laterna Magica"* on the portal pylons. Novák is also the creator of the unique and artistically remarkable "Mascarons" placed in the voussoirs of the fifteen semi-circled windows on the 1st floor of the front facade. These are large stuccoed allegorical heads provided in addition to floral ornaments together with a variety of tributes to the fields of Painting, Poetry, Science, Philosophy, Trade, Agriculture, Industry, and also Motoring and Aeronautics. The latter two are represented by two heads with hoods and protective glasses located above two side windows. Karel Novák is associated with other facade stucco work, these being colored and gilded city emblems, plastic floral ornamentation, vases and tombs, etc. on the front facade. Evidence of the same hand can be seen in the sitting figures of ephebs made of artificial stone and located above

 | 12

11 | *Antonín Štrunc: Allegory of Architecture*

12 | *Josef Mařatka: Allegory of Music*

13 |

the side-facade window ledges, etc. (not confirmed for all of the sculptures and elements). Other stucco elements on the side facades were created by **Antonín Mára** (south facade), **Eduard Piccart**, **Bedřich Šimonovský** and **František Kraumann** (north facade). A conspicuous feature which forms a continuous circle alongside the facade at the level of the 1st floor window ledges are plaques with deep three-quarter reliefs of semi-figures in folk costumes. This artificial-stone decoration showing the folklore of individual regions of Bohemia was created by a group of artists, which included **J. Pekárek**,

13 | *Back facade with a staircase tower*

A. Zoula, E. Piccardt, F. Kraumann, B. Šimonovský, A. Štrunc.

What most reminds one of an exhibition gallery is the line of huge figures erected along the building above the cornice. On the left corner of the front facade there is a symbolic sandstone sculpture of the *Spirit of History* with a sword by **František Rous**, on the right corner beside a spire there are figures made of artificial stone representing allegories of *Literature, Building trade, Sculpture* and *Painting* by **Antonín Štrunc**. The north facade is enlivened by an artistically interesting stone allegorical figure of a semi-reclining naked male "Drama" and a naked female *"Music"* by **Josef Mařatka**. The south facade is decorated above the attic window gable with a pair of stone figures depicting *Sower* and (female) *Harvester* by **Antonín Mára**. The exhibition of sculptures continues also on the lower levels of the building : At the level of the 1st floor on the front facade's left corner there is a portrait stone figure representing the Powder Tower's builder *Matěj Rejsek* by **Čeněk Vosmík**. The same corner just one floor below bears a memorial plaque from 1918 with a pair of allegorical figures by

14 | 

 | 15

14 | *Stucco decoration of the roof area*

15 | *Karel Novák: Allegorical Head, Commerce*

Ladislav Šaloun. The Western-side facade features a round turret with a spire on the corner which is enhanced by two fairy-tale figures *"Rusalka"* and *"Dudák"* of artificial stone by **František Uprka**. Another wonderful part of the facade is the stone decoration of the Neo-Gothic corridor connecting the Municipal House with the Powder Tower by **Antonín Štrunc** and **Josef Pekárek**.

| 16

16 | *Color mosaic above the doorway, created according to a painting by Karel Špillar*

THE MUNICIPAL HOUSE INTERIORS

THE GROUND FLOOR beyond the main entrance from Náměstí Republiky contains a lounge with marble wainscoting and an Oriental mosaic floor created by **G. Petrucci**. On the sides of the doors to the halls are two bronze reliefs representing *Fauna* and *Flora*, an excellent work done by **B. Kafka**. Light fittings and heater guards are a stylish addition left from the latest renovation.

17

On the right there is a FRENCH RESTAURANT, which has been kept close to its original appearance. The stucco decoration was created by **F. Kraumann** and his workshop, wooden wainscoting, boxes as well as original tables were all made by the firm **Ant. Baumgartl & Son**. In the main spacious room are allegorical scenes painted by **J. Wenig**, on a side wall there is a scene of *"Prague welcoming its visitors"*, on the left of the entrance to the elevated section is an allegory

18

17 | *The ground-floor floor beside a luxury elevator shaft*

18 | *Entrance Lounge with a bronze relief named Fauna (by Bohumil Kafka)*

19 | 

of *Hop-growing*, on the right is a *Wine-growing* allegory. On the wall in the upper section, original wallpaper was discovered and renovated. The painting *Western View of a Prague Evening* by **V. Tomec** was

20 | 

in 1938 replaced by the painting *Hradčany and Nový Svět in Spring* by **A. Zahela**. Light fittings made by **F. Anýž** as well as clocks were renovated and completed according to historical documentation. In the recesses of the windows new lamps have been hung, which were newly made according to the original ones which have not survived.

19 | *The French Restaurant*

20 | *The clock in the French Restaurant*

| 21

In the opposite half of the front section of the House, towards the Powder Tower is a CAFE furnished with original wainscoting, partition walls as well as mahogany partition tables with benches covered with leather. On the front wall in the Cafe there is a light fountain with a *Nymph* relief made by **J. Pekárek** of Carrara marble. The light fittings made by **F. Křižík** which had been devalued by later renovations were finally renovated according to the original documentation.

| 22

From the lounge one enters the STAIRWAY LOUNGE with an entrance wing to the Central Cloakroom. The Stairway

21 | *The Cafe is located on the ground floor*

22 | *Cafe — the fountain with a Nymph (by Josef Pekárek)*

Lounge also provides access to both of the main stairways leading to the basement as well as the upper floors. The terracotta floor by G. Petrucci has been renovated as well as other interior parts. On the side of the entrance door are an original cash register and a porter,s lodge and other equipment made by **J. Macoun**. The light fittings were made by **F. Křižík** and the luxury elevator cabins, today intended to be used by the president and the mayor only, were made by the firm **F. Ringhoffer**. The stucco decoration was created by **J. Čapek**.

23 

On the left of the staircase is an entrance to the NEW FOYER. This space serves among other purposes as a CULTURAL AND INFORMATION CENTER and a refreshment buffet. In the back it is connected with the Central Cloakroom by a newly built stairway.

THE MAIN STAIRWAY TO THE BASEMENT has ceramic wainscoting with decorative panelling and with scenes of historical Prague which have been implemented by the Rakovník factory RAKO according to the design by **E. Hlavín**. On the landing there are decorative reliefs by **A. Mára**. The metal hand-rails are precisely detailed.

In the BASEMENT the stairway is followed by a lower foyer with a ceramic-wainscoted fountain and an original ceramic ornamental floor. The light fittings are new. In the middle of the foyer there is

23 | *Lounge before the Central Cloakroom*

the entrance to the AMERICAN BAR. The bar was decorated with colored drawings by **M. Aleš** in the period 1910—1911. In 1921 these were replaced with copies made by **A. Neumann** of which six were in 1997 again replaced with new copies made by **R. Klouza**. On the

24 | 

pilasters decorated with replicas of original black ceramic tiles there are six drawings, these being : *"A cooper"*, *"A countrywoman with a goose"*, *"A (female) gardener"*, *"A butcher"*, *"A cook with a fish"* and *"A beater with a hare"*. In the boxes on both sides of the bar which was newly constructed according to old drawings there are the following scenes *"At the hunt"*, *"Arrival of a lord to a pub"*, *"Annual hop feasting in a pub"* and *"A carnival Tuesday"*. In the middle of the vault with gilded "rain" hangs an original chandelier with a drawing of *a heron*. The light fitting was made by **F. Křižík**. Other light fittings have not been preserved and are replaced with replicas. In the basement under the French Restaurant is the PILSEN RESTAURANT, decorated with three paintings by **J. Obrovský** which are in-

 | 25

24 | *The right-hand Main Stairway leading to the basement*

25 | *Ceramic wainscoting with decorative panelling along the stairway leading to the basement*

26 |

26 | *The American Bar is located in the basement*

27

serted within a ceramic mosaic: *"Harvest in Bohemia"* hanging on the wall by the bar and a *Boy* and a *Girl* beside a vaulted entrance into the elevated section. The damaged original furnishings by **J. Sadílek** have been renovated and completed with replicas including

28

the boxes by the windows, tables and chairs. Old drawings and documentation were used for making new light fittings and clocks. Ceramic tiles with city emblems as well as decorative window-panes are originals.

The decorative vases are reconstructions according to a sin-

27 | *The Pilsen Restaurant is located in the basement*

28 | *The Pilsen Restaurant — the clock in the hallway leading to the elevated room*

gle original which was preserved. Opposite the bar is a WINE-BAR where there is original wooden panelling, made by **J. Sadílek** with inset relief ceramic tiles and mirrors. Stucco decorations were created by **F. Kraumann**. The remarkable inlaid work around the small stage which had been mostly damaged is now restored as a replica of the original. Of the original light fittings only two lamps on posts by the entrance to the bar have been preserved. The chandeliers are replicas. Wall light fittings are a stylish new accessory. Particularly interesting are the original decorative window panes.

29 |

In the central part of the elevated ground floor is the CENTRAL CLOAKROOM, newly decorated, but with a high proportion of original furnishings still in use, namely metal hooks and mirrors on pilasters. A new terracotta floor has replaced the original ceramic floor. The wall light fittings are replicas of the originals which have not been preserved and the copies were created according to photographs from 1912. The

| 30

29 | *Wine bar — detailed view of wainscoting*

30 | *Wine bar — detailed view of pilaster ceramic panelling*

| 31

bars were newly manufactured according to the originals. The benches and ceiling light fittings are stylish new accessories.

The Cafe gallery continues into GAMING ROOMS with a corridor and a large pool-playing hall. It can be accessed also from a side staircase which can be entered from the street U Prašné brány.

The original furnishings which have not been preserved as

| 32

31 | *Central Cloakroom* 32 | *The Large Pool-Hall*

a whole include sections of wainscoting, frontal wall with mirrors in the pool-playing hall, heater guards and benches in the corridor as well as a furniture wall in the card-playing room. Here, as well as in the large pool hall, the light fittings were made according to the preserved drawings. Other furnishings have been made during the reconstruction in order to meet the demands of the contemporary function of gaming rooms but these were also inspired by the period documentation.

33

On the elevated ground floor, accessible from the street U Obecního domu there are CLOAKROOMS FOR THE ORCHESTRA MEMBERS. Of the original furnishings only doors and the corridor decoration with original light fittings by **F. Anýž** have remained. In the corridor, busts of the conductors *V. Smetáček* and *V. Talich* have been placed.

34

From the mezzanine to the upper floors lead the wings of the MAIN STAIRWAY with steps made of Carrarra marble and the balustrades made of Slivenec marble.

33 | *The elevator-shaft latticework at the Main Stairway*

34 | *Interior of the president's elevator*

35

35 | *The right-hand Main Stairway — the landing between the 1st and 2nd floors*

Stuccoes were created by **A. Štrunc**. Original light fittings which were made by **F. Křižík** have been renovated. The stairway is finished with original latticework around the elevator shafts, there are also notice boards, decorative window-panes and mirrors.

36 | 

The first floor is occupied by the MAIN FOYER with original light fittings, magnificent figural and ornamental decoration and with its walls covered by artificial marble. The foyer forms an entrance into the central space of the Municipal House which is the SMETANA HALL. The hall occupies the entire central section of the house and is several floors high. The hall, designed as a multi-purpose space, has on its front side a stage flanked by two stuccoed sculpture groups by **L. Šaloun** — *Vyšehrad* and *Slavonic dances*. The ceiling and wall

36 | *The Smetana Hall — view from the main entrance*

37 | *The Smetana Hall — view from the organ wall*

frescos — allegories of *Music, Dance, Poetry* and *Drama* were created by **K. Špillar**. On the balcony and box ledges there are plaques and portraits of the Czech composers *Jan of Holešov, Bohuslav of Čechtice, Kryštof Harant of Polžice and Bezdružice, Václav Jan Tomášek, František Škroup, Vilém Blodek, Karel Bendl* and *Zdeněk Fibich* by **J. Kalvoda**. Under the vault pendentives there are four sculptures by **K. Novák**, who participated together with **L. Kofránek** and **J. Kalvoda** in creating other stucco elements which can be seen in the hall. Woodwork and the woodcarved panelling of the stage was done by **J. Navrátil**. Some of the original furnishings include ceiling glass panes, lattice covering the air-conditioning devices, made by **A. Čada** and **J. Šimůnek**, mirrors, chairs in the boxes and light fittings, which were made by **F. Cvrk and the firm Suda Kotěšovec**. In the gilded lamps, set in long strings on the ceiling, the milky-tinted opaque glass was replaced in 1936 with the original cut glass. This arrangement was executed according to a design by **P. Janák**.

38 |

The hall is dominated by the organ, which was made by **J. Tuček**,

38 | *The Smetana Hall — the sculpture group Má Vlast/My Country (by L. Šaloun)*

39 

around which is a gilded-bronze relief of *B. Smetana* by **F. Hergesel**. The organ was renovated by the firm Vleugels, which is the successor of the original service sub-contractor to J. Tuček of the firm E. F. Wachler. From the National Museum collections the original organ bench was returned to the hall and was recently accompanied by a new electronic one. The original richly ornamented curtain and covers in the honorary boxes have been renovated. The decoration was completed by curtains on the doors and windows of the balcony. The chandeliers above the stage and balcony which were originally equipped with

 40

39 | *The Smetana Hall — a side balcony*

40 | *The Smetana Hall — view of the organ with the plaque of Bedřich Smetana (by F. Hergesel)*

| 41

41 | *The Mayor Hall with works by Alfons Mucha*

42 | 

arched lamps made by **F. Křižík** have been replaced by replicas made according to photographs taken in 1912.

The portal with the City of Prague emblem above the doorway connects the foyer with the MAYOR HALL containing **A. Mucha's** paintings. The ceiling fresco *"Slavic Concorde"* with an eagle in the centre is "carried" by eight pendentives on which human virtues are shown, personified by Czech historical characters : *Faithfulness* — J. A. Komenský, *Strength* — Vojtěch of Pernštejn, *Vigilance* — the Chods, *Intractibility* — Jan Roháč of Dubá, *Independence* — Jiří of Poděbrady, *Justice* — Jan Hus, *Maternal Wisdom* — Eliška of Premyslides, *Militancy* — Jan Žižka. The three wall frescos were inspired by the texts : *"Saint Mother of Nation, accept the love and enthu-*

42 | *The Mayor Hall — sitting box with decorative panelling by Alfons Mucha*

| 43

siasm of your sons!" "Humiliated and tortured you are but you shall be revived, my country!" "With strength towards freedom, with love towards concorde". According to Mucha's design doorway curtains were sewn by the students of the City Industrial Continuing School. The curtains have been preserved and renovated. Window-panes were designed by **A. Mucha** and installed by **V. Staněk** and **J. Šebek**. Original furniture provided with an interesting silver finish was made by **J. Krejčík**. Indirect lighting of the hall space was arranged to meet the proposal of **A. Mucha**. Two decorative panels, set in the heater guards above the sofas are replicas of the original colored drawings by A. Mucha. The original drawings can be seen at the Museum of the City of Prague.

| 44

The RIEGR ROOM with his bust by **J. V. Myslbek** is decorated by two frescos by **Max Švabinský** — *Spring in Bohemia*, 1913. In the lunette above

43 | *The Mayor Hall with the triptych "With Strength Towards Freedom, With Love Towards Concorde" (by Alfons Mucha)*

44 | *The Mayor Hall — detailed view of the window pane designed by Alfons Mucha*

45 

45| *The Riegr Hall*

46 | 

the doorframe are portraits of J. V. Myslbek, Mikoláš Aleš, Josef Mánes, Bedřich Smetana and Antonín Dvořák. In another lunette there are pictures of Svatopluk Čech, Jan Neruda, Jaroslav Vrchlický, Božena Němcová and Julius Zeyer. Original wall panelling as well as furnishings by **J. Navrátil** have been renovated and finished with embossed gilding. There is a plaque in the wall, with a text of Riegr's arguments at the Czech Kingdom Assembly gathering on May 25, 1867. The library which is located in this room is crowned with a Prague allegory by **J. Pekárek**. The stucco ornamentation was created by **A. Štrunc**. The light fittings in the room are originals, the embroidered covers and upholstery have been re-made according to old photographs and little fragments of the original material.

 | 47

The SLADKOVSKÝ HALL, originally named the Lecture Hall, has been preserved in its

46 | *The Riegr Hall — bust of F. L. Riegr (by Josef Václav Myslbek)*

47 | *The Sladkovský Hall — the entrance to the Riegr Hall*

48 | 

original appearance including wall panelling and light fittings. Around the stage there is highly unique, renovated wallpaper which is intended to imitate silk. Above the heater guard with a lattice made by **A. Čada** is a painting of a landscape by **J. Ullmann**. *Dr. Sladkovský's* bust has been returned to its place in the hall. The bust was created by **L. Kofránek**. Stencilled paint-work has been reproduced to match the original appearance.

In the wing beside the street U Obecního domu, there are DINING-ROOMS, a set of four rooms, connected by sliding doors with colored door panes, with original wainscoting, mirrors and clocks. The wallpaper used there was newly manufactured according to the fragments of

 | 49

48 | *The Sladkovský Hall*

49 | *The Sladkovský Hall with fireplace latticework on the stage*

|50

50 | *The Western Dining-room — the mirror wall with a clock*

51 | 

the paper that were found. The light fittings are made to a sensitive new design.

The room which was previously used for preparation of meals has been made into a sitting room, matching the style of the dining-rooms. A painting of *Český Krumlov* from the collections of the Municipal House by **A. Liebscher** now hangs here.

Between the Mayor Hall and the Grégr Hall is the PALACKÝ HALL with decorative canvases by **Jan Preisler** made 1910-1912, installed on the walls and the ceilings. Between the windows is a bust of *František Palacký*, created by sculptor **Myslbek**. The bust is placed on a marble pedestal. The light fittings in this hall are originals and were supplied by **F. Křižík.**

 | 52

The GRÉGR HALL, originally called the Debating Hall, is decorated by a ceiling fresco triptych—*Life*, *Poetry*, and *Death*, dating from 1911 and three later paintings, *Love Song*, *Battle Song* and *Burial Song*.

The paintings were hung there in 1914. These canvases

51 | *The clock in the Western Dining-room* 52 | *The Palacký Hall*

53

53 | *The Grégr Hall with František Ženíšek's paintings*

54 | 

were created by **F. Ženíšek**. The walls are covered with artificial marble laid to an intricate design. On the pier between the windows there is a bust of *Dr. J. Grégr* by **E. Halman**. The stucco decoration was created by **A. Novák**. The balcony hand-rail used to be decorated by a cover which has not been preserved. The original light fittings and chandeliers were made by **F. Křižík**.

From the hall stage a CORRIDOR LEADS TO THE POWDER TOWER. The corridor was recently arranged to accommodate gatherings.

Inside the wing facing the street U Prašné brány there are a row of rooms for social meetings, called the Ladies, Debating Rooms.

 | 55

THE ORIENTAL ROOM, which was originally called the Serbian Room, still has the original stencil paintwork and ornamental stucco decoration with in-set colored glass. The furnishings, along with benches, window panes and the recently completed chandeliers which previously had some elements missing, have been preserved, including cush-

54 | *The Grégr Hall — inset marble wainscoting*

55 | *The chandelier in the Oriental Room*

ions and some curtains. Their present appearance follows that of 1912.

The adjacent BOŽENA NĚMCOVÁ ROOM has a fountain in a mosaic-tiled recess. The fountain was created according to **O. Polívka's** design. The ceramic pylon is decorated with a subtly-glazed sculpture of B. Němcová, recently re-made according to a photograph.

Through the doorway we can walk into the MORAVIA-SLOVAKIAN ROOM which is decorated with an enchanting painting with original embroidered lambrequins, accompanied with hand-weaved curtains with beads. Original furnishings in the room include the wall-panelling, leather-covered benches, marble table tops and chandeliers. A unique period accessory is the aquarium. The leather-upholstered armchairs were recently made according to an old photograph.

56 | 

The largest room of this wing is a FORMER CONFECTIONERY with a rich stucco decoration and mirror walls and original light fittings. On the pillar at the alcove, there is a painting by **V. Jansa** showing the town of *Tábor*. Other original fittings in the room include glass cabinets, benches, several tables with gilded footrests and marble tops as well as the lower part of the counter. The upper part of the counter has been renovated according to old drawings as well as the chairs and tables.

56 | *The Božena Němcová Room — the fountain*

57 

The adjacent CONDUCTOR'S ROOM was created by converting the former kitchens, whose ceramic tiles with floral ornaments have been covered by wainscoting. The room's furnishings originate from 1996—1997.

The CORRIDOR BESIDE THE RIEGR AND SLADKOVSKÝ HALLS, with the mirrors and doors with allegorical wooden relief panels above the threshold, is connected with a second corridor beside the dining-rooms which has original light fittings and mirrors.

The corridor just before the Grégr Hall has copper lamps and furnishings by **J. Macoun**, and connects with a corridor alongside

57 | *The Oriental Room*

|58

the rooms and confectionery. This other corridor has original wall-panelling and a sofa, made by **J. Bělík**. The wall-paper is an almost identical replica of the original.

From the corridors near the side entrances to the Smetana Hall NEW STAIRWAYS have been built, leading to the side boxes and balconies. The new entrances are positioned in place of the original mirrors, which have been removed and are now in the performers' dressing rooms.

On the SECOND FLOOR in the wing leading towards Náměstí Republiky (the Square of Republic) is an UPPER FOYER with stuc-

58 | *The Moravia-Slovakian Room*

59 | 

coed sculptures beside the entrances to the main balcony of the Smetana Hall, with an original round table with a marble top. In the opposite wall there is the portal into the HOLLAR HALL which is a circular room with a glass ceiling and silver-plated light fittings. The hall is connected on both sides with the EXHIBITION HALLS which are equipped with upper lighting, original light fittings and curtains around paintings.

 | 60

In the SECOND MEZZANINE there used to be the GATHERING and CLUB ROOMS. In the wing facing the street

59 | *Confectionery — view of the front wall*

60 | *The Big Exhibition Hall with the exhibition "Intimate Space/New Distance — Art of Prague Art Nouveau" (May 3—October 19, 1997)*

U Obecního domu, in the former rooms of the gentlemen's club and agrarian club, there are now two memorial plaques commemorating the events of October 28, 1918.

The plaque by **J. Šejnosta** (1921) with the portraits of the so

| 61

named "Men of October 28th": F. Soukup, A. Rašín, A. Švehla, J. Stříbrný and V. Šrobár was designed by **V. Hofman**.

The plaque bears a text written by historian J. Pekař : "*This room witnessed the making of history, here in this room the National Committee held its meeting, awaiting the fall of the Austrian empire and making preparations for Czech liberation. Here on the triumphal day of 28 October 1918 the committee took over the power of the Czech lands, here Komenský's words*

61 | *Conductor's apartment in the attic above the stage*

fulfilled : ,The rule over your matters shall be returned to you, Czech people.'"

In the next room of the gentlemen's club is a plaque commemorating the take-over of military power by the National Committee. The sign says : *"In this room of a gentlemen's club, where the Czech will, Czech suffering, Czech defiance and Czech belief had been expressed through the friendly concorde of the government members from the very first day of the*

62 |

World War, there between the evening hours of 8 and 9 o'clock on the grand day of our history of 28 October 1918, the former Austrian military power of the 8th army corps was taken over by the National Committee."

On the upper floors where there used to be flats, laundries, etc. there are now offices. The space in the back of the house serves now for performers' dressing rooms and the technical facilities of the Smetana Hall. There is also a new rehearsal room here and in the former attic is a large apartment with a view of Prague Castle.

62 | *Memorial plaque commemorating the events of October 28, 1918 (designed by V. Hofman, created by J. Šejnosta)*

Published by the Enigma Publishing House, Ltd.

for Prague's Municipal House.

Enigma, Ltd., Tolstého 16, Praha 10

Conceived by / Nataša Hrádková

Contributors / Ondřej Šefců, Věra Müllerová, Pavel Jerie

Editorial Consultant / Marie Platovská

Translation / Romana Kempná

Graphic Layout / Robert V. Novák

Typesetting / R.V.N.D.B.

Managing Editor / Roman Paleček

Photographer / Věroslav Škrabánek, AMP Praha (3), NTM Praha (4, 5)

ISBN 80-902327-5-2

| 63

63 | *The Palacký Hall — ceiling fresco (by Jan Preisler)*